Copyright © 2024 Paul Bright

All rights reserved.

No portion of this book may be reproduced in any form without written permission from the publisher or author, except as permitted by U.S. copyright law.

This publication is designed to provide accurate and authoritative information in regard to the subject matter covered. It is sold with the understanding that neither the author nor the publisher is engaged in rendering legal, investment, accounting or other professional services. While the publisher and author have used their best efforts in preparing this book, they make no representations or warranties with respect to the accuracy or completeness of the contents of this book and specifically disclaim any implied warranties of merchantability or fitness for a particular purpose. No warranty may be created or extended by sales representatives or written sales materials. The advice and strategies contained herein may not be suitable for your situation. You should consult with a professional when appropriate. Neither the publisher nor the author shall be liable for any loss of profit or any other commercial damages, including but not limited to special, incidental, consequential, personal, or other damages.

Book Cover Design by Samantha Carr

Table of Contents

Introduction
Disclaimer
How Sleep is Supposed to Work
The 12 Steps

0.   Commitment
1.   Hype Up with Sol Power
2.   Nutrition for the Mission
3.   Quiet on the Set
4.   Caffeine Boundaries
5.   Dress for the Occasion
6.   Exercise your Sleep
7.   Delayed Sleep Gratification
8.   Replenish the Brain
9.   Tension Release
10.   Drop The Thermometer
11.   Turn Off (Almost) All The Lights
12.   Don't Think About Sleep To Sleep

Introduction

I am a Certified Sleep Science Coach. I do sleep well — but it wasn't always that way.

I didn't become a Certified Sleep Science Coach until five years AFTER (mostly) overcoming two decades' worth of some pretty scary sleep disorders. You may have had the same experiences, including:

- Waking up in the middle of the night with a tight chest, not sure if I'm going to breathe properly again

- Going to bed at random hours and sleeping well until an overwhelming feeling of being buried alive happens over and over again until I can will myself awake

- Being so afraid of these first two experiences that I stay up as long as I can to avoid them and then pass out from exhaustion, only to have them happen anyway

- Irritability and inability to focus on even small things

- Always losing my keys and even missing easy turns on the way home

It all started at the beginning of my military career and didn't end until many years after. Yes, getting educated and certified in sleep science helped me understand the "why" behind all things I ultimately did to help myself, but I could have saved myself a decade or so if I knew it back then!

That is what brought me to writing this book.

I want to take all my education and experience to help you reset your sleep within months, rather than over a decade like it took me. I want you to reset and maintain your good sleep without relying on medications, over the counter pills, or potions.

I didn't want to just give you a dozen sleep hygiene tips randomly pulled from the Internet. I wanted to present 12 essential, highly effective sleep hygiene practices and habits, with an explanation as to "why" they work, how to use them, and when to use them to discover what works best for your sleep. These are the ones that I've found work best for busy people like you that want to improve sleep on your own first.

Our daily life, especially in the busy Western world, doesn't do a good enough job teaching us how to sleep. This becomes more evident as our life responsibilities shift or we have a drastic change in schedule that disrupts your healthy sleep routine.

It took me years, but after I built a strength-based, holistic approach, my clients significantly improved their sleep in as little as *two weeks*. That system is designed for one-on-one or small-group cohort work, but the 12 steps in this book were derived from it and can still help you.

Most of my clients are people juggling increased work responsibilities and don't have the time or money to pay for prescription medications that only work for a little while. Others are military veterans like me who didn't learn good sleeping habits while serving and now want to snooze like a civilian.

If you fit these categories, this book is for you. Sometimes people like us just need to be pointed in the right direction!

Now, let's get real. Notice how the title doesn't read "12 EASY steps" or "12 GUARANTEED steps" or "12 QUICK steps"? It's because they aren't easy, guaranteed, or quick — but they do work, as long as you keep doing them and adjusting where necessary. Consistency is key, just like with any major lifestyle change you want to maintain, be it getting out of debt, losing unhealthy weight, or moving up the ranks in your job.

If they were *easy*, everyone would already be doing them with no problems! Sleep recovery gets tough because there is often too much information out there with not much explanation as to why things work; or the information is for very specific circumstances and won't work for someone who just needs redirection and a hand-up.

If they were *guaranteed*, everyone who reads this book would be 100% committed with no life interruptions. Staying consistent will help you get back on track faster if you get *off* track. I used to have weekly sleep paralysis attacks; they are now maybe six times a year because it is so much easier to recover and get back on track due to my consistent sleep schedule.

If they were *quick*, they wouldn't lead to permanent or long-lasting positive results. You would get a boost in your sleep for a week or two, and then back to the same problems you had before. It would be like crash dieting where you lose weight but also lose key nutrients in the process.

Follow the 12 steps. Apply them in order as much as you can and strive to do them every day. Most steps take less than 15 minutes to incorporate into your daily life. The hardest part is staying consistent with your newly developed habits, but even that will get easier over time. I also believe, as I learned through my client work, that some of these steps you are already doing successfully and don't even know it! Learning the "why" just makes them easier to do every day! If you're interested in the deeper science, I have a page at the end that includes the scientific publications I used to help create this book.

Let's start the 12-step journey toward the sleep you deserve!

DISCLAIMER

Although methods in this book are science-based and have had positive results, the information here is for educational purposes. Results may vary. These methods are not intended to diagnose, treat, or cure sleep problems that could be the results of clinical mental health or medical disorders. If you have one, or suspect that you do, please consult your physician.

How Sleep is Supposed to Work

I add this before any class, any book, and any lesson anyone wants to glean from me.

Just like you can't walk until you learn how feet move, you can't reset your sleep until you know how sleep is supposed to work.

It's like putting together a 500-piece puzzle without knowing what the end product will look like.

The first thing you must learn is that the sleep cycle begins *when you wake up*, and not when you decide to go to bed! This is the start of your circadian rhythm.

Your eyes contain hormonal triggers (retinal ganglion cells) that let your brain know it's time to wake up and be alert. They also signal the brain it's time to produce serotonin, a mood-stabilizing hormone that reduces anxiety and depression by helping you keep an even-keeled mood. The production starts when sunlight hits your eyes, and the blue photons trigger the brain into synthesizing tryptophan, the precursor to serotonin.

Adenosine is a hormone that slowly builds up during the day and releases when the sun goes down to let you know it's time to get ready for sleep.

Cortisol, a stress hormone, starts producing in the middle of the night. It peaks during midmorning and energizes you like a "kick start," but not at a fight-or-flight level, and is usually out of your system by sun-down.

Melatonin is produced by serotonin and tryptophan, but its release is inhibited by sunlight or bright lights on the skin. It starts to transition from the middle of your brain and spread into your bloodstream around 9pm, when the sun is completely down. It makes you very sleepy.

Once you get to bed, the sleep cycles begin.

Stage 1 is the light sleep, when you start yawning and shut your eyes. You are edging into deep sleep. You can still be easily awakened or disturbed in this stage.

Stage 2 is the beginning of deep sleep, where your body is practically catatonic and in a state that nothing can trigger your senses to immediately wake you. A catatonic body also prevents you from rolling over and falling off the bed. Your breathing becomes shallow and your body's core temperature starts to drop.

Stage 3 is a deep recovery stage of sleep, when growth hormones release to repair and rebuild your cells, including those in the muscles. Your immune system also starts rebuilding in this stage. If your body is healing and rebuilding with no other systems interfering, it's going to be more difficult to wake you!

Stage 4 is the REM (rapid eye movement) stage when your memories are sorted through. Your brain decides which ones to keep and which ones to toss out. This is often where dreaming happens.

The stages cycle three to five times a night and last approximately 90 minutes for each cycle.

This is the basic sleep design for your body. A number of other physical and environmental cues can also affect your quality of sleep, including vitamins, minerals, external factors, and internal systems. You will learn more about these in this book.

The 12 Steps

Step Zero: Commit to a Bed Time!

I don't include this as an official step, because the title says it all: commit to a bed time.

No matter how much effort you put into studying the following steps, it will be much, much harder to build them into your daily and nightly routine without a committed bed time.

You may feel like you're failing the first few nights, or even week, of committing to a time and then hopping into bed and then STILL having trouble sleeping. That's normal. But committing to that time, no matter when it is, will help associate your body with restorative sleep.

It doesn't have to be an exact minute, or even 15 minutes. But do your best to tell yourself "Whatever I do, I'm going to be in my bed within 15 minutes of (insert time here)."

Why is commitment so important? If you depended on the timely taking of medications to cure a severe illness, how often would you miss them?

Sleep is not life-or-death in one night, but it does wonders for your health and quality of life in so many ways.

Do you brush your teeth at the same time every day and night? Likely yes. Your teeth won't fall out if you miss a day, but the more you can maintain your routine, the healthier your teeth and gums are for the rest of your life. Eventually your bedtime will be the same way. You go to bed at the same time every night without conscious question because it's part of your life routine.

This was the first thing I did when I started winning the battle against sleep paralysis. I got over the fear and of anticipating it happening, and just said "eff it. I'm gonna be in bed by midnight NO MATTER WHAT." The first week was rough. But eventually my body began to accept, anticipate, and crave sleeping before the midnight hour!

If you KNOW you're staying up way too late, don't set a time that's three hours earlier. Start *one* hour earlier, then scale back as necessary. Do this first, and everything else will fall into place. Eventually you will take actions within the 12 steps that help you glide into that target bed time. Soon enough, your strict bedtime will expand into a flexible window, plus or minus a half hour. Your routine will become so normal that for days you get "off" track, you get back on track much faster. I've been there, done that, and now I wake up with no alarm clocks. But it starts with committing to a bedtime.

Step One: Get Adequate Sun Exposure

Your sleep cycle doesn't begin when you close your eyes. It begins at sunrise.

If you remember those childhood summers spent running around all day outside, you might not remember how quickly you went to bed once the day was done. That's because the sun kept you happy and triggered a set of internal processes that promote good sleep and growth!

Yes, good sleep actually starts when you wake up — and the best start happens when you wake up with the sun in your face. The bright ball of gas in the sky is responsible for getting you ready for sleep 18 hours before your head even hits the pillow!

It's easy to forget how good the sun is for us. As of this publication, we're coming out of a two-plus year pandemic where people stayed indoors much more than usual. I would argue that, before the pandemic, daily sun exposure was already down, outside of scheduled vacations.

How interesting is it that when we think about vacations, we aren't imagining going to grim, dark places for two weeks. Nope! Whether it's the forest, a beach, or the mountains, we want to be out in the sun. It makes us happy.

So, let's recognize how that works for us, biologically, in sleep and in mood.

Multiple scientific studies note that the amount of sunlight you need is based on skin color and time of year. Fairer skinned people can benefit from up to 15 minutes during

Spring and Summer without significant risk of skin damage and 30 minutes during the Fall and Winter months. Darker skinned people should double or triple that amount of time.

You don't have to lay out and tan for this type of sun exposure. You just need enough to expose your arms or legs. You can do this through general outdoor activities like walking or yard work.

The right amount of sun intensity or illuminance is key. It is typically measured in lux (lx), which is a unit of illuminance. Lux is defined as one lumen per square meter (lm/m^2), where a lumen is a unit of luminous flux.

The lux level can vary depending on factors such as the time of day, weather conditions, geographic location, and atmospheric conditions. On a clear day, outdoor sunlight can have an illuminance of around 100,000 lux or more. However, this level can decrease significantly during cloudy or overcast days. A bright light in your room might put out 750 Lux, at best. On a clear day, the sun can put out 10,000 Lux around 7am. That's a minimum amount of sun exposure required to get the optimal benefits, so long as the UV Index is between 3 and 5. Beyond 5, you can risk burning yourself.

Getting that direct sunlight on your eyes (without blinding yourself!) can start your body's production of serotonin, which improves your mood. A good mood reduces responses to stressors that can pile up all day and affect you through the night. Beta endorphins are another set of calming hormones that sunlight exposure helps to produce and release.

This exposure also starts the ball rolling for production and release of melatonin, which helps you get sleepy at night. More steps in this book will outline exactly how that works.

If you can't get direct sunlight in the morning, consider purchasing a special light box that can emit at least 10,000 Lux. These light boxes have timers that gradually control the increase of light exposure. If you get one, have it pointed towards your face's usual direction when you wake up. One meta study analysis showed that even artificial sunlight therapy can show significant improvement in mood, sleep quality, and hours spent sleeping.

Who doesn't like free stuff that's good for you? And if you can't get the free sunlight but have to purchase a light box, that's a very small investment for a lifetime's worth of benefits. Get that Sol power!

Step Two: Eat A Nutritious Breakfast

10 years of military-style meals did me no long-term dietary favors. It did, however, do the service a favor because I was able to get proteins and carbohydrates very quickly into my body and put them to use immediately.

Yet it didn't leave much time to digest my food and get the most out of all the other nutrients I needed. Coffee and a biscuit were a quick breakfast, either on the way to work or right before bed. If I had an extra five minutes, maybe I could suck down some eggs and orange juice.

Serving the country also means that serving yourself breakfast can happen at odd hours. A majority of my military career was spent starting work between 3 and 7pm; and ending at either midnight or 7am. So breakfast was usually at a normal person's dinner or late-night snack time!

What I learned over time was that I needed to not rush breakfast; I needed to embrace it and use it to wake my body and mind for the day. Breakfast became one of my best friends for helping reset my sleep, especially once I started eating the right things.

When I transitioned to non-vampire hours I started eating a more balanced breakfast. It was a slow path to travel but, again, I was learning on the fly and learning it the hard way. It took some extended research about vitamins, nutrients, and amino acids to help get me straight. Let me start by telling you what I learned about vitamin D.

Vitamin D

Vitamin D plays an important role in many, many functions of your body. D2 can be obtained through produce but it doesn't synthesize as fast as D3, which can be derived from animal products or the sun exposure mentioned in Chapter 1.

One lesser-known function of vitamin D is its relationship with inflammation. It has been shown to suppress the production of pro-inflammatory cytokines, including Tumor Necrosis Factor-alpha (TNF-α). Some studies in peer-reviewed journals suggest that vitamin D deficiency may lead to increased TNF-α levels, potentially contributing to chronic inflammation and various health issues.

Elevated TNF-α levels are associated with inflammation, which can disrupt sleep patterns. Chronic inflammation has been linked to sleep disturbances, including insomnia. Vitamin D's role in reducing TNF-α levels may indirectly promote better sleep by mitigating inflammation.

For your sleep cycle hormone and neurotransmitter production, vitamin D is responsible for converting tryptophan into serotonin, which keeps your mood more positive and in turn, reduces the stress-induced hormone cortisol, which is expected to be out of your body by bedtime. Higher levels of cortisol can also keep you up at night since it is part of your fight-or-flight response.

Tryptophan is an amino acid you often hear about being in turkey and milk. It's also in tofu, nuts, chicken, and oatmeal, to name a few sources. Getting 1.8 mg per pound of your body weight should be enough to help produce serotonin, while

600 IUs of vitamin D is recommended. Foods high in Vitamin D include trout, salmon, mushrooms, soy, and 2% milk.

Vitamin D is also in the pathway of melatonin secretion and production. When it's about 9pm, or when the sun has completely left the horizon, no matter the time of year, melatonin releases from your pineal gland (located deep inside your brain) and into your bloodstream, causing that drowsiness effect when it's time to hit the hay.

If you recall the earlier chapter on how sleep is supposed to work, remember I mentioned that your body's core temperature drops and you also go nearly catatonic? Melatonin is responsible for helping regulate those processes.

So, a quick recap: getting vitamin D helps boost the mood, which reduces stressors that can keep you up. It also helps melatonin do its job promoting deeper sleep.

Yet vitamin D can't do it all alone. It needs help from magnesium, a mineral that helps your body make Vitamin D available for use.

Magnesium
Magnesium's strength also comes into play in its involvement in a multitude of your body's systems — Over 300 functions, in fact! One of its chief functions is to keep your cells cool when you're in deep sleep by regulating their operating speeds. Cooler cells signal the body that it's time to release the regrowth and repair hormones.

This also includes regulating GABA, the amino acid that helps your brain power down for sleep.

Magnesium's other sleep function is to help control your muscle's nerves. To keep yourself from getting hurt in your sleep during the deep stages, your muscles have to stay as still as possible, aside from the ones responsible for breathing, blood-pumping and brain function. It's one reason why people who suffer from Restless Leg Syndrome can benefit from magnesium supplements. The glycinate and citrate versions are best. Magnesium glycinate is more easily absorbable and promotes good REM, while magnesium citrate is better for relaxing your nerves before sleep.

When you pair it with magnesium, you create a dynamic duo! Magnesium works best at night, while vitamin D is best absorbed in the day.

B Vitamins
B1 helps cells convert carbs into energy, which contributes to your wakefulness when you're supposed to be awake instead of grogginess when you're not. B3 and B6 play critical roles in regulating cell speed and keeping your body's temperature cool during the restorative sleep part of your sleep cycle. Salmon, chicken, chickpeas, and bananas are good sources for both vitamins.

B9 and B12 are involved with producing serotonin. Low levels of B12 have been associated with Restless Leg Syndrome.

Sleep Better With A Better Breakfast
You can get great sources of magnesium in common breakfast foods! The recommended daily allowance is 400-420 mgs (milligrams) per day for adults. One typical serving of

fortified breakfast cereals contains 42 mgs. A packet of instant oatmeal has 36 mgs, while a cup of low-fat plain yogurt contains 42 mgs. Those giant shredded wheat blocks? Two will net you 61 mgs!

Non-dairy milks are a great vitamin D source. 600 IUs are recommended daily and most non-dairy milks can get you anywhere between 100 and 144 IUs per cup.

By now you could be off to a good start with resetting your sleep, and it doesn't even require a wholesale schedule change! Think about combining the efforts from the first two sections. Have breakfast in direct sunlight and incorporate meals that are rich in vitamin D and magnesium. That makes the next step in resetting your sleep even more beneficial: meditation.

Step Three: Meditate

Meditation helps get the mind ready for sleep — and not just at night!

You might associate meditation with Tibetan Monk chanting. One of the reasons the chanting works is because it forces your mind to focus on one singular rhythmic activity and it's driven with a simple physical action. I can imagine that if you do this enough, a mind that's "all over the place" finds a sense of calm.

But meditation isn't just about invoking chants and chiming bells. There's nothing wrong with all that, but it isn't practical for everyone.

As busy as you are with many responsibilities, meditating for 15 minutes could net you an amazing return on investment. It might seem counterproductive because it involves setting aside time. Yet, the value you gain with every minute after is almost limitless!

Meditation helps with dopamine and serotonin production. If you can start off your day this way, you may already be loose and balanced enough to take on any challenges, rather than running into them headfirst.

However, nighttime meditation can also be beneficial. Scientific research also suggests that meditation increases melatonin potency.

Since there are no known substances that increase melatonin plasma, it is theorized that meditating for a minimum of 30 minutes slows down blood flow and therefore, slows down melatonin metabolism.

Being loose and relaxed gives you better insight and a more methodical approach to problem-solving without stimulating that fight-or-flight response that can exhaust your body, yet keeps your mind running, even after you close your eyes.

All you need for meditation is a quiet place where you can engage in an activity that requires almost no thinking and no distractions. It could be pacing around your garden. It may be listening to the ocean. It might even be folding your laundry! Whatever you can do to take time to yourself and pause the brain without sleeping can count as a healthy meditation.

You have to be intentional about it. Don't try to just fit it in your day whenever you can. Instead, build it into your day as a regular activity, the same as you would with brushing your teeth or attending any important appointment. Schedule around it. Don't let it be an option.

My form of meditation happens in the morning when I make coffee. I prefer to make French press-style coffee because it takes longer.

Yes, I like my coffee slow, homemade, and deliberate. Making French press-style involves creating a coarse grind for a stronger flavor. I inhale the aroma of the grind while I boil hot water in an electric kettle that has a nifty blue light.

I put the grinds in the French press. When the water is just past the boiling phase, I pour just enough to cover the grinds, inhale the steam and aroma, and let it steep for two minutes.

Then, I pour the rest of the water in and put the press atop it and let it steep for another 5 minutes. When the time is up, I slowly press and force the hot water even further into the grinds, releasing the oils and natural flavors.

A leisurely, steamy pour into my porcelain coffee cup is next. From there, I let the aromas swirl around my nose even more and take that first sip. It's a good 15 minutes of prep and 15 minutes of sipping in my own alone time that gets my good, happy hormones flowing for the day. I don't think about anything other than making that coffee and enjoying it. That is meditation for me.

Now that you know about meditation's benefits, here are a few different meditation methods you can engage in.

Prayer To A Higher Power
Whatever your beliefs are, a higher power tends to be a source of comfort and strength. Focusing on praying to that higher power in the morning may help stimulate those positive hormones and at night, may settle your mind before bed.

Gentle Instrument Play
Almost any instrument will be good for meditation purposes, so long as you are going with the flow and not trying to compose a song or even the craft. Just play freely and let your mind embrace the sounds and feelings. If you have no instrumental playing experience, consider getting a small drum or chimes. You need virtually no skills to get the meditation benefits from playing them.

Binaural Beat Music
Binaural beat music is music with special rhythms that are designed to regulate your brain wave's oscillation speeds. The rhythms are nearly subliminal and can regulate those speeds to relax or energize you. It's one of my favorite ways to meditate. I play these beats through quality noise-canceling headphones.

Body Mindfulness
Body mindfulness is taking time to focus on your body parts or senses. You can do progressive muscle relaxation, where you contract muscle groups for a few seconds and then relax, starting with the top of your head and progressing towards your toes.

Fixed focus is also a form of body mindfulness. You can engage and recognize your senses by picking a serene object or scenery and concentrating on how your senses respond to them. My coffee meditation is a form of body mindfulness, from how the beans smell to the vibration of the grind.

Speaking of coffee...

Step Four: Monitor Stimulants

This is probably one of the more well-known sleep improvement tips: limit your caffeine intake.

However, there are other stimulants besides caffeine that can impact your sleep. And there are other sources of caffeine besides coffee that, if you aren't on the lookout, can affect your sleep!

Caffeine Beyond Coffee
You might already know that too much caffeine can keep you awake. That being said, understanding the "how" and "why" behind this can help you set limits and enjoy it properly, as I described in the last chapter.

Coffee should be enjoyable in the morning. It can help you stay awake and alert and get your blood pumping. This alertness can boost the "happy" endorphins!

But coffee, or more specifically, caffeine, needs to be limited in consumption or it can disrupt your sleep cycle. Also, in case you were wondering, there IS a clinically diagnosable condition for caffeine addiction.

For you non-coffee drinkers, you might not have a caffeine-free diet. Tea, soft drinks, energy drinks, and chocolate all contain levels of caffeine.

My biggest caution would be pre-workout supplements and drinks. Consuming these for any workouts after 12pm could have a lingering effect in your brain well into the night. Without adequate deep sleep, all the damage done to your muscles will be deprived of repair and regrowth needed to get the gains.

Caffeine Versus Adenosine

Adenosine is what I call the "clock watcher". It's a hormone responsible for managing your sleep-wake cycle. It accumulates throughout the day and then releases at the proper time (generally when it gets dark outside) to help your body get sleepy. The more energy you expend, the more adenosine builds up in your system. Adenosine releases later in the evening to put on the finishing touches.

Caffeine blocks the reuptake receptors of adenosine so that you don't get sleepy. When you drink a caffeinated beverage, its effects start to peak within an hour. Caffeine's half-life, or when it is half-strength, can be anywhere between 5 and 9 hours, depending on your genetic makeup. An 8-ounce cup of coffee typically has between 80 and 120 milligrams of caffeine. At 300 milligrams, you can start to feel the jitters. When the caffeine wears off, you can get super sleepy because of the adenosine build up flooding your system now that it's allowed to enter the receptors.

Imagine you wake up at 8 am and have two cups of coffee by 10 am. 200 milligrams of caffeine should be fully hitting you around 11 am. If you don't have any more caffeine after that, it will be halfway out of your system between midday and after dinner, possibly around 6 pm. At the latest, you'll have eliminated the caffeine in your body by 10 pm, or an hour after melatonin release. Your brain can go into full rest mode because it's got nothing keeping it up at that point.

The later you ingest caffeine, the later that timeline extends for your brain. Ingesting caffeine after 12 pm means it's still well within your system at midnight. Even if you want to go to sleep and close your eyes, your brain is still ready to solve calculus problems. You wake up groggy, which pushes the need for more caffeine.

Thus, you may not need to drop coffee or caffeinated beverages altogether. Think about how much you are getting and when you are getting it. Don't forget that certain foods, like darker chocolates, also have caffeine! Those late-night morsels could spell disaster for your sleep cycle.

Tyramine, Tyrosine and Ginseng
There are more naturally occurring stimulants that could also be keeping you awake. *Tyramine* is a naturally occurring substance that, when broken down by enzymes, can produce norepinephrine. Norepinephrine increases blood pressure and heart rate. Moderate amounts of tyramine should be fine but if you eat foods with higher amounts close to bedtime, you could be in for a long, sweaty night. Aged cheeses, processed meat, and smoked fish all contain high levels of tyramine so consider other fresh and cool high-protein sources.

Tyrosine is an amino acid derived from another acid called phenylalanine. It also naturally occurs in foods, with higher concentrations found in foods such as sesame seeds, cheeses, and milk chocolate.

Tyrosine is actually good for you in moderation and helps promote alertness by promoting dopamine production. That said, remember that having high concentrations close to bed can make you too alert to sleep.

Ginseng is another good food source that regulates your nervous system. Some people even replace their coffee with ginseng tea because the concentration and energy boost is much more even-keeled. If you are going to drink ginseng tea or take supplements, you may want to avoid doing so before bed to avoid experiencing those stimulating effects as you're preparing for a restful sleep.

None of these chemicals and substances have to be completely eliminated if you are resetting your sleep. You just need to be mindful of when you're consuming them and how much you consume.

Step Five: Change Clothes

Have you ever noticed how you can hold your bowels for a long time, but as soon as you get near a bathroom door, you feel like you're going to explode?

That's because your body has, over the years, associated those restroom doors with relief. Your brain has established a visual cue for a physical function.

You can do the same, at an even deeper level, to improve your sleep. You do it through very important wardrobe changes. It starts by getting out of your work clothes as soon as you get home.

I was notoriously bad about this during my military service. I would take off my uniform jacket, but leave my t-shirt, pants and boots on until just before bedtime. As soon as I woke up, it was a quick shower and then into 3/4 of my uniform again until work. When I separated after 10 years, I had clothes in my closet that looked new but had been worn maybe three times a year. My body rarely knew what it was like to *not* be at work.

Even when I became a civilian, I didn't change out of my work clothes until before bedtime, save for my shoes. I still carried that bad habit. Once I switched to my "three outfit" technique, it was easier to get my mind and body ready for bed.

The first outfit is your *work outfit*. You pick it out the night before so that you don't have to rush into your day. It takes less time to choose an outfit after dinner versus trying to get it together when you've only got 5 minutes to get out of the house and make it to work on time.

When you get home, make getting out of those clothes one of the first things you do. Even if you work remotely, continue the act. Change out of your clothes once you get off the clock!

You will change into the second outfit: *your leisure clothes*. This could also be your gym wear if you plan to work out. A coworker of mine used to call his leisure pants "`my eatin' pants." They were his cue for a good, fulfilling dinner! Either way, it should be significantly different from your work clothes, but not a set that you sleep in.

The last outfit is your *sleepwear*. You put this on maybe an hour before you go to bed.

You don't need high-tech sleepwear made of rare materials to get your best sleep. If it's made of breathable material like cotton, that's a good start. Even more breathable are bamboo-sourced materials, like viscose.

Sleepwear should also be very loose and not cause any undue tension that inhibits circulation. Poor circulation can cause soreness in your muscles and extremities. Trust me, it's not a fun way to wake up in the middle of the night!

Also consider avoiding any thick caps or footwear. Your body dissipates heat as you go into deep sleep. Your body's core temperature drops so that it can begin its restore and repair cycles. Those cycles burn fat and generate heat, which mostly escapes through your feet and head. If you restrict those escape points too much, you can find yourself sweating at night.

All of these outfit changes can also apply to remote workers, home business owners and stay-at-home parents. It's much easier to skip these changes when we work from home because there's no environmental change to naturally prompt a clothing change.

However, it's likely more important for you than anyone else! Consider setting calendar reminders, or even laying out your "leisure" and "sleep" clothes before you hit the home office.

If you're working from bed, please avoid that as much as possible. I hinted at this in Step Zero, and more detail will follow in Step Seven.

This sort of consistency will keep the mind and body aligned as to "what" you are supposed to be doing "when."

Step Six: Work Out Your Sleep

Exercise is another component to helping reset your sleep. Just make sure you pick the right kinds for the right time.

Vigorous exercise at least three times a week does more than just physically exhaust you to the point where you want to pass out on a jogging path. These workouts will boost your endorphins and blood flow. The endorphins keep the stressors down, while the blood flow improves the cell restoration and repair during your deep sleep periods.

It's also a healthy distraction from any mental stressors you're experiencing!

Focus on the Exercise
One thing I have shied away from as I've gotten older is multitasking. It's efficient for short periods of time, but in the long run, it's added burnout for your brain. Exercising should be no exception.

I recommend that you don't do any sort of work while exercising, i.e., talking work on the phone during your afternoon walk, talking work with coworkers in the gym, etc. Just work out and be in the moment, whether it's painful or enjoyable.

Even regular, not-so-intense exercise, is good for your sleep. You're still activating your muscles and promoting positive blood flow throughout the body. A nice, scenic walk can put a smile on your face and relax you. Your immune system gets stimulated and your mind winds down.

Timing Is Everything
Be careful as to how much you exercise before bedtime. Your body is designed to drop its core temperature while you sleep. As soon as you hit stage 2 of sleep, that core temperature lowers a few degrees, which is the cue for your brain to release your growth hormones.

By exercising too close to bedtime, you raise that temperature and interrupt your sleep cycles. Recent research studies have shown that exercising with moderate intensity close to bedtime actually can increase your core temperature during sleep! Consider stopping all exercise at least two hours before bedtime.

Exercise, Mood, and Sleep
If you find that your mood gets more negative at night, there's research to support it. Unprocessed emotional events that happen during the day have a way of coming out after midnight when you are alone and awake. This can disturb your sleep and overall mood.

Conversely, while it's best to handle these emotional situations during the day, you don't always have that option and it can impact your sleep and mood late at night.
This is where morning exercise helps. Endorphins are short chains of amino acids (proteins) produced naturally by the body. These neuropeptides are synthesized and released primarily by the pituitary gland and the hypothalamus in the brain.

The endorphin release you get from morning exercise can help keep your mind at peace all day, which helps you ease better into bed at night.

Also, cortisol isn't always a bad thing. There's a cortisol boost that keeps you alert when you engage in vigorous exercise, and you don't want that boost taking place while you drift off to sleep.

When possible, take it a step further and exercise out in the sun first thing in the morning! If it's quiet, you will likely have fewer distractions. You'll get the sun exposure we discussed in Step 1 and get the full endorphin boost that carries you into the night!

Regardless of when you exercise, make it a point to do a proper cool down. Change out of your gym clothes as soon as possible to let that body heat escape. A mild temperature shower and cold water throughout the day after your workout can also help you.

Step Seven: Avoid the Bedroom

Have you ever had a favorite restaurant you saved for those special holidays and occasions with friends and family? If so, that special spot has memories tied to it and likely evoke nice, happy thoughts.

You already know that even if you can afford to go there weekly, it loses its magic.

Your bed should have virtually the same effect on your body. The minute you go horizontal on it, your body should have one of two expectations: sex or sleep. Keep that in mind when you wake up in the morning. Other than those activities, avoid your bed at all costs!

It's not much different than when you hold your pee during a road trip. Your bladder seems to have no limits but as soon as you see the door to a restroom, you feel like the dam may burst any second. Your body has trained itself to respond to a physical cue.

In this case, you create the sleep trigger physical cue by avoiding the bed until the time comes. Don't nap in it, eat in it, watch TV in it, do your homework — anything other than sex or sleep.

To Nap or Not To Nap?
One of my nightshift clients asked me this question. She took naps during the day to help her recover from working all night and doing all her house responsibilities. She preferred to stay awake from around 3 am until at least 7 pm, with a

nap in between. It was completely understandable to crave a nap but she didn't want to mess up her sleep cycles.

If you have to or want to nap, you don't want to nap longer than 20 minutes. That's short enough to get a good body reset but not long enough to manipulate yourself into thinking you are going into a deep sleep. If you nap too long, you could risk disrupting your sleep at night because your body already thinks it has started into restorative sleep when it really didn't.

Try to find somewhere comfortable that isn't your bed — even the floor is a good spot. It might be just comfortable enough to fall asleep, but not so comfortable that you end up waking once you try to turn over.

If you absolutely, positively must be in your bed for a nap or anything else, don't get *too* comfortable. Keep your regular clothes on. Use an alternative blanket. Sit up in the bed versus laying down on it or getting under the covers. I became an unwilling expert at this in the military. I had to learn how to take naps in the strangest of arrangements and positions. You don't have to be a military veteran to do this!

Step Eight: Improve Hydration and Time Your Digestion

One of the surest ways to improve your sleep quality is through brainwashing.

No, not listening to subliminal message tapes or joining a cult, but through proper hydration. It can save your sleep AND your memory.

Your brain is 70 percent water. It also can generate the equivalent of 20 watts of energy via the electricity generated through thinking and running your life systems!

At night, it needs cooling and re-hydration, especially during cell restoration and repair during those restorative sleep hours.

Yes, you naturally lose water through the day from urination and sweating. But you also lose water just through breathing — between 300 and 400 milliliters a day. That's a glass and a half just from existing!

Part of those night time brain repairs include your memory restoration. It's theorized that during your REM sleep stages, your brain is sorting out what memories to keep and what to toss out, which could be why your dreams can feel mixed up and convoluted! The dead cells are supposed to get washed away with a mix of water and cerebrospinal fluid.

When you are dehydrated, the fluid is less effective in removing the dead cells, leading to plaque formations in the brain. These plaques are very similar to plaques seen in

Alzheimer's patients. If you plan to preserve your memory, hydration becomes more important as you age.

In short, if you want to keep your memory, it's best to stay hydrated! Drink plenty of water during the day. Drink some at night, but not too close to bedtime, or you will break your sleep cycle to urinate. Nutrition experts recommend an average of 64 ounces a day, broken up throughout the day. Your total water intake, to include food, should be 125 ounces for men and 91 ounces for women. There will be some give and take to these amounts based on your weight and general health, so check with your physician.

Hydration is also an effective way to help remove toxins from your body. Toxins like lactic acid and ammonia can build up and impede blood flow via muscle tension. Drinking water helps dilute these toxins throughout the day so that there is less built up by night.

When you wake up, drink a glass of water because your brain has likely used up a lot of fluid during your sleep cycle. If you wake up sweating, drink even more!

If you are one of those "I hate water" people, there are alternatives, like fruits and vegetables. Cucumbers, watermelon, strawberries and celery are more than 90% water! Each serving also gives you fiber and electrolytes, which helps keep some of your body functions going. You likely won't "eat" your way to full hydration, but consuming produce is a "bang for the buck" alternative.

Other nifty ways to stay hydrated are with coconut water and infused waters. Also consider having soups or broths as a meal. Herbal teas can be a great post-dinner hydration

finisher. Loose leaf teas have almost no calories but are chock full of stress-reducing nutrients. Just look out for caffeine levels in them!

I also wouldn't recommend maintaining hydration through sports drinks or soft drinks. Sports drinks are beneficial for athletes because they are actively losing electrolytes. Even soft drinks that are zero calories contain chemicals that your body has to process in addition to hydrating your body and brain.

The water content in a soft drink varies depending on the type and brand. On average, a standard 12-ounce can of soda contains about 90% water. The remaining percentage consists of dissolved sugars, acids, flavorings, and carbonation.

It's important to note that while soft drinks contribute to overall fluid intake, they often contain added sugars and calories, which may have health implications when consumed excessively.

It's easy to mistake these types of drink as hydration sources because they are liquids typically consumed with a meal. The closer you can get to nature with your hydration needs, the better for your body.

The Final Meal

The timing of your last drink and meal also has an impact on your sleep. Your last meal should take place no later than two hours before bed.

I interviewed Toussiant Stewart, a whole foods expert and gut health expert, on my podcast. We talked about the digestive system and he told me about the three stages. The last stage of digestion takes place two hours before bedtime. That's when all of the food is completely broken down, and the nutrients are released into your bloodstream.

These nutrients include those that aid in recovery and repair. If you eat any closer than that and go to bed, your body will still be "working" instead of "resting". You'll lessen the chance of waking up with heartburn or needing to use the restroom.

One of the worst offenders is alcohol. Alcohol will make you drowsy and make you think that you're getting good sleep because you'll pass out. However, your body works very hard to get rid of it while you are getting a quick snooze. Remember that Rapid Eye Movement stage where your memory forms? Alcohol disrupts it.

Your liver sees alcohol as a poison, so it gets activated and works overtime to expel it through your waste system.

And people tend to have a harder time going back to bed when awoken from these alcohol effects.

You're better off stopping drinking four hours before bedtime if you don't want the alcohol to get in the way of your sleep recovery.

Step Nine: Stretch and Massage

My injuries incurred during military service were not the result of combat or significant accidents. They were incurred over time and had built up from repetitive stressors. My knee and ankle on one side had been significantly compromised from imbalance carrying. My toolboxes were heavy — up to 100 pounds for the big jobs!

My lower back damage was a result of... everything. I was 32, with eight years of working on the flight line, when I bent over to pick up a golf ball and couldn't get back up. The doctor told me I had, "the back of a 50-year-old." I rehabbed it enough to get through the rest of my service, but as you get older, everything hits different. (On a side note, I write this book as I turn 50, and I now officially have the back of a 50-year-old.)

Your sleep can suffer from these types of injuries. Having a supportive pillow or two to neutralize your spine is something that does help, but even more helpful is a combination of total body stretching and massaging.

What I learned through all my physical therapy is that the body's entire muscle structure is connected in some way or another. Big tension in your calf can go up a chain and pull on your back. A shoulder injury can impact your wrist. Your body will compensate for all of these injuries and interruptions as you stand — but when you lay down? The dynamics change and you could find yourself tossing and turning all night because that's when your back decides it's had enough of trying to hold everything together.

To help eliminate this (assuming you've cleared it with your doctor), consider a total body stretch before bed and address any tight spots and increase blood flow. Even if you don't have significant injuries, a physical day can build up lactic acid in the muscles, which contributes to soreness that you don't feel until you finally lay down.

For home-based workers, take time to stretch and move all your major body parts frequently. Build it into your schedule for 5 minutes every hour of sitting/standing.

In addition to stretching, consider some self-massage. Massage can break down scar tissue and increase blood flow throughout the body. I have learned to use therapeutic massage guns a few days a week.

With the massage gun, there's less stress on my own body for an effective tension release. I use the gun on my notoriously tense spots, like above my knees or my soles. I also work the massage gun on any major muscle group I work out on that day, whether I am feeling pain or not. The massaging stimulates recovery and less pain during sleep.

My other daily tool is a medium density foam roller designed for deep tissue. It has special textures and divots that reach deep into the large muscle groups. I roll my back on it nearly every night for five minutes. Again, it helps with improved blood flow and pain relief for easier sleep.

Here are a few other tension release methods and options that may be a good fit for your mental and physical needs. They require meeting with specialists on a schedule that works best for you.

Acupuncture
Yes, it involves needles. But these needles are perfectly placed in body parts called pressure points along meridian lines which, in theory, control energy flow in the body. Depending on where your tension is, needles are placed on the right points to release the tension.

Trager Massage
This is a massage technique that involves gentle movements and stretching as dictate by how you communicate your responses and feelings to the practitioner. This may be good for people who experience tension and are not sure exactly why it's happening, or can even pinpoint where it's happening.

Rolfing
Rolfing massage practitioners conduct 10 sessions of deep tissue massage. They focus on different areas each time to create tension release. The ultimate goal is to create any needed structural changes between your muscles and skeletal system. If you've had a change in job types and are experiencing pain a few months after the transition, this might be for you. I wish I would have known about Rolfing when I went from working on the flight line 12 to 14 hours a day, to working behind a desk and barely moving 8 hours a day!

Whatever method you choose, self-induced or with help, stretching and massaging will promote relaxation and circulation for better sleep.

Step 10: Sleep in a Cool Room

The best way to eat ice cream is when it's cold.

You won't hear much argument against that. Yes, technically, you could eat warmer ice cream but it can get sticky and you may end up drinking it more than eating it.

This is the analogy I think about when it comes to sleeping. Your body sleeps best when it is cool versus when it's warm.

Yes, you can fall asleep at relatively warm temperatures if you are tired enough from a long and draining day. You may even sleep through the night. However, there is a negative impact on your body's ability to recover and restore.

As mentioned earlier, your body's temperature naturally drops during sleep in stage 2 so that in stage 3 your body knows it's time to start discarding old cells, rebuilding damaged ones, and growing new cells where needed. If external temperatures are too high, it makes the cool-down process harder, therefore the repair or regrowth process may be hampered.

Help your recovery by keeping the room cool. Optimally, you may wish to set your room temperature anywhere between 68 and 72 degrees Fahrenheit (20 to 22 Celsius) for sleep.

For those of you who live in naturally warmer climates, I understand the struggle. I spent most of my childhood in the Philippines, and most of my tweens and teens in either California or the southern United States. I'm no stranger to heat! Living in those places often meant the "low" temperature of the day was in the 80s. But your body gets accustomed to it, so you can make a relative temperature adjustment and get the same benefits. Maybe 68 to 72 degrees is a hard target, but 74 to 78 can give you the same relative effect.

An added benefit of cool sleeping, for those trying to lose unhealthy weight, is that fat burns more during cold sleep. The healthy "brown" fat, which takes up less space, starts to use the "white" fat as fuel to warm up the body as needed.

If you sleep in a large room, consider starting the cool-off long before you go to bed via fans, air conditioning units, etc. Keep hot devices off the bed. Consider more breathable bedding or pulling the thick covers back before sleeping. Also remember to heed advice from the "Avoid the Bedroom" chapter and keep your body heat off the bed.

You may also want to get more localized by getting a specialized temperature controlling device for your bed. They plug into a blanket or mattress to evenly cool or heat your sleeping environment, even before you put your head to the pillow. They can be pricey but a worthy investment, especially if your bedroom or overall environment's temperature is in the extremes.

Your bedding also needs consideration. Choose natural, breathable materials like 100% cotton or bamboo to help dissipate body heat.

Now that the room has cooled off a bit, it's time to put on the finishing, sleep-inducing touches: darkness and quiet.

Step 11: Sleep in a Dark and Quiet Room

A dark room is the best room for sleep. Not just "kind of dark" or "mostly dark," but, "I can barely see my fingers in front of my face," dark. It is the natural circadian rhythm trigger and if all goes well up to this point, you won't even realize the level of darkness for long; You'll be in stage 1 sleep as soon as your head hits the pillow!

At the start of this book, we discussed how sunrise, blue photons and UV rays help let your body know it's time to wake up and be active. The opposite is just as true. When the sun goes down, your body's adenosine hormones let you know it's time to work towards sleep.

Around 9 pm, it should be dark enough to let your pineal gland know it's time to release melatonin and make you really sleepy. If you were outside in nature while this was happening, the likely level of light you would see may be from the stars, the moon, or fireflies — and that is just from looking up. Looking at ground level, you might see the equivalent of a candle's light.

In modern times, how much artificial light do we view after 9 pm? Think about the luminescent power of overhead lights, TV screens, phone screens, and even Christmas lights! Remember in Step 1, I noted that a bright room light produces 750 Lux? A candle emits only 10.

There is still hope for those who want light to feel more secure. Some research suggests that LED lights in the right spectrum can provide lighting but not interfere with melatonin release.

To help reset your sleep, start turning down or turning off all those lights as it gets later.

When you get to bed, turn over any clock lights. Turn off bathroom lights. Close those curtains tight or, in some cases, get blackout curtains. Yes, it will seem like it's pitch-dark and may be a little frightening — But if you turn off all those lights and close your eyes for 30 seconds, you can open them again and your mind will adjust to the darkness. You will be able to see enough to get out of your bed, if need be. You can even use a small night light by the door; just keep it out of your eye's natural view path when you sleep. That way, it doesn't accidentally wake you should you turn over or open your eyes between sleep cycles.

With respect to past trauma or anxiety, it can be hard for some people to sleep in the complete dark. I will always encourage you to continue to get the professional help you need to help with those issues. Anxiety and other mental health concerns can certainly interfere with sleep but it doesn't mean you can't improve it while getting the help that you need.

In the meantime, consider at least trying to scale back the amount of light you need to comfortably help you get to sleep. Also remember, all is not lost if you can't! You will learn in the following pages that not every step has to be done 100% for you to reset your sleep. This may be one of the steps you have to work around more.

It's Oh, So Quietish

Remember how I wrote that in Stage 1 your sleep is light enough that your senses are still active? You'll return to that stage a few times in the night and it's possible that ambient noises can affect you every time you're back in Stage 1.

Achieving the "quiet" for your sleep may require some experimentation if it's not something you've already established. What is overlooked is the need for quiet not just for the onset but the entire duration of your sleep to avoid those interruptions.

Getting total silence as you sleep can be hard to get. My personal belief is that it feels like the best option because in deep sleep, we don't seem to hear anything. Yet the help is more needed in between cycles, so some sort of tolerable background noise is more helpful. Some people like music. I love music, but I start singing along and can't sleep. Others love podcasts. So do I, as long as they are semi-boring. As a military dependent and a veteran, the sound of cargo planes flying overhead used to be comforting to me.

As long as the background noise isn't too stimulating, it can help. The following are descriptions of background noise types that may help you.

White noise is often referred to as "pure" or "flat" noise. It contains equal energy across all frequencies, making it sound like a consistent hiss, similar to the static on a TV when it's not tuned to a channel. White noise is often used to mask other sounds and promote concentration or sleep. In the therapeutic world, we use white noise makers outside of doors to mask private client conversations.

If you prefer white noise, you can get both background noise and a cooler room by investing in a small fan!

Pink Noise has more energy in the lower frequencies and less in the higher frequencies compared to white noise. It sounds deeper and is often described as a gentle, consistent rumble. Pink noise is sometimes used in audio testing.

Gray noise is similar to white noise but is adjusted to sound more balanced to the human ear. It may be perceived as smoother and less harsh than white noise.

Red noise, sometimes called brown noise, has less energy at lower frequencies compared to white noise. It is characterized by a softer, more gentle sound, often described as a distant waterfall or wind in the trees. This is one of my preferred background noises.

Green noise is less common and has a more complex frequency distribution. It may sound like a mixture of various natural sounds, such as rustling leaves and water flowing. This is another preferred background noise setting for me.

Now your room should be set up like a mysterious book character: Cool, dark and silent. The final step in resetting your sleep is getting your mind right to embrace it.

Step 12: Relax Your Thoughts

This last step is likely the most important step of all. It absolutely belongs at the end of the steps because it's the last thing I want you to think about: not thinking about sleep.

You do this by mellowing your thoughts as much as possible so that you don't even realize you are going to sleep. No matter if you do all the other 11 steps right during the day, or 10, or 5, this last one, relaxing your thoughts, has to be done the most consistently for it to work.
Reign in your brainwaves and you'll be naturally ready for sleep.

Brain Waves and Electricity
We know your brain is the most powerful part of your body and requires a lot of energy to operate. Every command, cell movement, and thought happens so fast that it generates measurable electricity and heat.

This electricity oscillates at different speeds, depending on your activities. In fact, your brain can generate enough power to turn on a 20-watt light bulb!

Beta waves show your brain is at work. These are the second-fastest waves. When you're working, trying to solve a complex problem, or even engaging in stimulating conversation, you can produce beta waves.

Alpha waves show your brain at idle but awake. Activities like folding laundry, watching mindless TV, or singing a familiar song encourage alpha waves. They help give your brain a rest but keep you alert for the next beta wave activity.

Theta waves are pre-sleep waves. They are also present if you are very relaxed and in deep thought, like through meditation as shown in step 3.

Delta waves are present during deep sleep. If you've been able to accomplish all the sleep steps and made it to bed, your stages 3 and 4 of sleep will show more delta waves.

Gamma waves are the fastest waves. They can represent deep cognitive thought and alertness.

There are studies that indicate manipulating your brain waves to promote more Alpha and Theta wave activities can reduce anxiety symptoms! [12]

Ideally, before bed, your brain should slow down enough to produce "Theta" waves on an EKG machine. In deep sleep, you would see more Delta waves.

Yet, you can't get to the Theta waves of initial sleep in a matter of minutes.

If you go to bed but you are thinking about work, life strategies, or worrisome events, you could very well have Beta waves and Gamma waves showing up, which generate enough electricity to keep you out of deep sleep. Even fun and creative thinking before bed can do this!

Yes, on the surface, it can be like saying, "don't think about a pink pony," which causes you to think about a pink pony.

But hear me out.

One of my favorite clients is a very busy mother-of-two who worked two jobs. Her days began at 6am, taking the kids to school and onto her home-based business. Then she'd pick her kids up, eat a quick meal, and then off to her second job. She'd get home, have dinner, and be done by 9pm, but would stay up talking to her friends until 3 in the morning! It was the FOMO "Fear of Missing Out" with friends and leisure time that created this pattern.

It was exhausting. For eight years, she was on this schedule!

Initially, her overall goal was to be in bed by midnight. It wasn't something she wanted, but felt she needed, because she was a zombie with her kids and jobs.

My assessment of her via the four domains (body, nutrition, bedroom and mind space) determined she could absolutely accomplish this within three months if we put in the right interventions and build onto her already existing strengths, like her bedroom. It was already dark, cool and quiet once the sun set.

One of my assessment questions unlocked the biggest change. I asked her when was her last good night's sleep.

"It was with your meditations," she answered.

I had sent her a binaural beat meditation I designed to help our brain waves slow down and ease into sleep.

Although my client hated the thought of going to bed at midnight, she enjoyed having meditation time. So in her personalized journal, she put "Meditation" in place of "sleep" at midnight.

That halfway worked for two weeks. She went to bed around 1 am. A significant improvement, but it wasn't the goal. She felt disappointed, but I reminded her that change doesn't happen that quickly, yet she had increased her nightly sleep from three hours to five within two weeks!

And in the next two weeks, she hit her midnight goal.

A month later, she told me she was finding herself in bed by 10pm!

Within two months, she tackled her biggest obstacle — the mindset before bed— and went from three hours of sleep to seven. There were a few other factors that helped, but wow! More than doubling her sleep hours with the right mindset is something I would consider a huge success.

You can do the same as she or I did or begin navigating your own path to a more restorative sleep.

I listen to semi-boring podcasts most nights. They are just interesting enough to keep me distracted from my thoughts about the day or the external sounds at night. You see, those years of military living still had me on the "edge" every night at bed. I no longer needed to live that way, but my brain had not caught up. Having a healthy distraction to cover those little sounds is a big help. Within 15 minutes, I am lights out!

Another coach/client I worked with expressed that she still liked to read and scroll online before bed. The problem was that most of her reading material stimulated her creative brain and therefore, the online scrolling stimulated her argumentative side! Neither was conducive to helping her stay asleep.

So, our plan involved stopping work several hours before bed and to only read non-stimulating material. She went from waking up several times a night with thoughts, to barely waking up once a night within three weeks. A month later, she told me that although her solid sleep nights aren't perfect, there was a vast improvement. She reported, "I actually fell asleep faster than I used to and now when I wake up, I go right back to sleep." This has improved her mood at work, thus improving her interpersonal relationships.

Consider what you can do before bed to not think about' sleep. If you use audio products, consider setting them on a timer to automatically shut off. Follow my client's planning process and work to reduce or stop working on activities that encourage Beta and Gamma waves hours before bed.

Try not to use music that you will end up singing to — this has backfired on me since I love to sing!

If you use social media sites, be wary of the screen lights keeping your eyes up even though the music is peaceful. Also consider any audio sources that include disruptive ads.

I am not going to lie. This is likely the hardest step to take and will not happen quickly. It might take days or weeks but there will be progress and before you know it, you won't even remember hitting your head on the pillow.

In fact, keep Step 12 in mind with every other step before it. Relax your thoughts as you build each one to your needs. Don't spend too much time wondering if they work and getting stuck with paralysis by analysis. They work. You'll find a way to make them work!

Congratulations!
You reached the end of the book and now you are more armed and ready to improve your sleep! 12 steps, backed by science and experience, to help reset your sleep, will keep your memory sharp, your mood positive, your immune system thriving, and your overall quality of life improving one night at a time...doing almost nothing with your eyes closed!

Keep coming back and working these steps as necessary, and you'll see those added minutes turn into hours. Before you know it, you'll be getting the sleep you want AND deserve!

A Restorative Sleep Schedule

I hope you found some great insight with the 12 steps to reset your sleep!

I'm sure you were already doing some of the right things, just as I was when I decided to take control of my sleep and get back on track. Now, it's just a matter of building off of your strengths and creating the discipline to start on the steps you never knew about!

The truth is that you don't even have to do every step every day to get your sleep back on track, but you won't really know that until you try them all. Most take less than 15 minutes to incorporate. The nutritional support is a matter of reading labels and making appropriate switches. Some steps, like setting up your sleep environment, only take a few adjustments that become permanent and also become your baseline if you change environments and need to set up a new sleep sanctuary.

Having said that, you are probably wondering "is there a perfect sleep schedule?" Yes, and no. Yes, there is an ideal you can aim for, like an ideal balance of diet and exercise —But no, the reality of life is that everyone has different challenges. And yes, having an ideal sleep schedule is something to aim for. And no, you may not reach it perfectly.

An Example Restorative Sleep Schedule

6:30 am	Gentle stretching, curtains opened, sunlight in. Meditation. 8 oz. water
7:00 am	Light 30 min workout, 8oz water, shower.
8:00 am	Breakfast w/ rich sources of vitamin D, B, Magnesium, 8 oz. water or 2 fruit servings
10:00 am	5-10 mins stretch, 8 oz. water
12pm	Lunch (D, B, magnesium), 8 oz. water or a fruit serving. Cut off from caffeine sources
3pm	5-10 min stretch, short walk, 8 oz water
5:30pm	Home, change into "leisure" clothes, 8 oz. water OR change into "gym" clothes, work out.
6pm	Dinner (rich in magnesium) OR 6:30 after gym.
8pm	Cut off time from food and drink
9pm	Turn off/ reduce lighting throughout home; engage in relaxing activities; change into sleepwear
10pm	All lights off, curtains closed, gentle stretching
10:15pm	In bed, Pre-sleep peaceful sounds

Whether you use this exact schedule or a personalized one, the general principles remain the same: having something consistent and feasible to build off of will help build a sleep foundation you can return to if you get off track.

Thanks To...

- My family and friends for supporting me through this journey!

- My focus groups for providing real-life evidence, support in your skills, and encouragement to document my journey and help me help others. It's always a good thing when you can come on Line and Share Our Support with each other!

- My clients who, through trial and error, inspired me to make necessary changes and absorb your strengths to grow my own.

- Rachael Landau – all the bleeding, virtual red pen edits I asked for, you gave, and then some!

- Sammy- thanks for your cover design! I couldn't have asked for a better cover that matches my message. If anyone's interested in having her make a cover for you, you can contact her at samcarr@gmail.com

References

These are some of the resources I used to create this guide. Many mechanisms of sleep are still largely unknown to even the most experienced sleep researchers. However, there are some commonalities in results among many studies.

Feinberg, I., & Floyd, T. C. (1979). Systematic trends across the night in human sleep cycles. https://doi.org/10.1111/j.1469-8986.1979.tb02991.x

Mead M. N. (2008). Benefits of sunlight: a bright spot for human health. Environmental health perspectives, https://doi.org/10.1289/ehp.116-a160

Radiation: The ultraviolet (UV) index. (n.d.). https://www.who.int/news-room/questions-and-answers/item/radiation-th e-ultraviolet-(uv)-index

Lindskov, F. O., Iversen, H. K., & West, A. S. (2022). Clinical outcomes of light therapy in hospitalized patients - a systematic review. https://doi.org/10.1080/07420528.2021.1993240

National Institutes of Health. (2017). Dietary Supplement Fact Sheets. Nih.gov. https://ods.od.nih.gov/factsheets/list-all/

Lim, L.L. (2019). What a Pain! My Childhood Leg Cramps Are Back. Sleep Disorders. https://doi.org/10.1093/med/9780190671099.003.0030

Tooley, G. A., Armstrong, S. M., Norman, T. R., & Sali, A. (2000). Acute increases in night-time plasma Melatonin levels following a period of meditation.
https://doi.org/10.1016/S0301-0511(00)00035-1

Sweeney, M. M., Weaver, D. C., Vincent, K. B., Arria, A. M., & Griffiths, R. R. (2020). Prevalence and correlates of caffeine use disorder symptoms among a United States sample. Journal of Caffeine and Adenosine Research
https://doi.org/10.1089/caff.2019.0020

Aritake-Okada, S., Tanabe, K., Mochizuki, Y., Ochiai, R., Hibi, M., Kozuma, K., Katsuragi, Y., Ganeko, M., Takeda, N., & Uchida, S. (2019). Diurnal repeated exercise promotes slow-wave activity and fast-sigma power during sleep with increase in body temperature: a human crossover trial. Journal of Applied Physiology
https://doi.org/10.1152/japplphysiol.00765.2018

Vandekerckhove, M., & Wang, Y. (2017). Emotion, emotion regulation and sleep: An intimate relationship. AIMS Neuroscience, 5(1), 1–17.
https://doi.org/10.3934/Neuroscience.2018.1.1

Tubbs, A. S., Fernandez, F. X., Grandner, M. A., Perlis, M. L., & Klerman, E. B. (2022). The mind after midnight: nocturnal wakefulness, behavioral dysregulation, and psychopathology.

Ding, Y.-S., Carvalho, V., Storey, P., Frew, D., Pizinger, T., Jackson, K., & St Onge, M.-P. (2018). Brown fat activation, sleep restriction and obesity. The Journal of Nuclear Medicine
https://www.tandfonline.com/doi/full/10.4161/temp.29120

Lu, C.-C., Chou, C., Yasukouchi, A., Kozaki, T., & Liu, C.-Y. (2016). Effects of nighttime lights by led and fluorescent lighting on human Melatonin. Journal of Ambient Intelligence and Humanized Computing, 7(6), 837–844. https://doi.org/10.1007/s12652-016-0383-2

Dadashi, M., Birashk, B., Taremian, F., Asgarnejad, A. A., & Momtazi, S. (2015). Effects of increase in amplitude of occipital alpha & theta brain waves on global functioning level of patients with gad. Basic and Clinical Neuroscience. https://www.ncbi.nlm.nih.gov/pmc/articles/PMC4741268/

www.ingramcontent.com/pod-product-compliance
Lightning Source LLC
Chambersburg PA
CBHW070413230526
45471CB00006B/2780